MW00522729

Pails Scrubbed Silver

Pails Scrubbed
Silver

Sandra Duguid

*To the Wonderful Staff
of my Hometown
Library!
Warmly,
Sandra Duguid*

NORTH STAR PRESS OF ST. CLOUD, INC.
St. Cloud, Minnesota

ISBN: 978-0-87839-644-3

First edition, March 2013

Printed in the United States of America

Printed by
North Star Press of St. Cloud, Inc.
P.O. Box 451
St. Cloud, MN 56302

www.northstarpress.com

For Henry
For my sister and brothers: Carol, Al, and Don
and In Memory of my sister Joyce
and of my parents, Mabel and W. Elton Duguid

Acknowledgments

Acknowledgment is made to the following periodicals and other sources for poems that first appeared in them (sometimes in a slightly altered version):

America: "Road to Emmaus"
Anglican Theological Review: "Forerunner," "The Pledge," "Tapestry"
Buffalo Spree: "The Giraffe"
Christianity and Literature: "Memorials," "Lord, Let Light," "Trek"
The Connecticut Writer: "This Is the Picture of Mother on the Path Between Our House and Store"
Ethos: "A Genre Painting"
For the Time Being: "Hat," "Nineteenth-Century Dream"
Journal of New Jersey Poets: "The Usual"
Lyrik Und Prosa: "Dream," "Summons"
Modern Poetry Studies: "The Occurrence (Almost)"
Poetry Now: "The Primitive Portrait Painter Addresses Her Daughter"
Radix: "Inland, Lancaster County"
Stonework Journal: (Online literary magazine, Issue 3, 2007, Houghton, NY): "Be," "Can You Imagine," "Property," "Reading a Student's Paper"
West Branch: "Role of Nonsense," "Sampler"
The Worcester Review: "Why Forrest K. Moses Didn't Enjoy Painting on Pottery, Though He Did It for Family and Friends"
"Miss Weld" was published in *The Country of the Risen King* (Grand Rapids: Baker Book House, 1978).
"Stories from the Southern Tier" was published in *On Turtle's Back: A Biogeographic Anthology of New York State Poetry* (Buffalo: White Pine Press, 1978).
"At Christ's Birth" and "This Christmas" were published in *A Widening Light: Poems of the Incarnation* (Wheaton, IL: Harold Shaw Publishers, 1984).
"End of a Job" appeared in *Missing Spoke Press Anthology* (Issue 6, Summer 1999)

Contents

I

II

III

I

Can You Imagine

Can you imagine
what good fortune
has brought you here
to this bright deli in Livingston?
Eggs blossom on your oval plate
by browned potatoes;
you are eating a bagel—You.
And there's no reason
this couldn't be
a breakfast room in Paris,
and you, the painter many disdain
for his failure to include
in his glorious morning interiors
more of the sinister.
And there's no reason
this couldn't be Bailey's Mills,
and you, your grandmother,
jealous, early on, of your mother
for having more children
than she ever even knew,
while she had only
one boy—your father.
Even so, you'd like to think
in some way—
when the sky hung down like her long skirt
that she could still pick up and move—
she was thinking of you
with kindness
when she sent him across the snowy fields
and roads to the one-room school
with his sandwich,
and then labored to paint
morning glories up either side
of the runner on the stairs
of the big house
that's no longer there
where trains picked up
and left off their passengers
over by The Junction.

The Primitive Portrait Painter
Addresses Her Daughter

It's not true, love
that we paint
stock
bodies in the cold
lull of winter
(when the sap gathers to the roots
of your father's maples)
and then go out searching for heads
to complete the picture:
that's a rumor,
had it never been started
would have been better;
no, get a face first in spring,
when the hills to their farms are easy to climb
and sun flashes on wood and pail.
Paint every wart,
every wrinkle and fault;
no smooth, godlike looks
sleeked over triangular bone
as though nothing had been suffered
or, perhaps, won;
come home by early summer,
gather the ripe and irregular
berries to deepen the color,
there still will be time
to add a suitable
body
later.

A Genre Painting

We were all
sitting in the Sear's Old Fashioned
breakfast nook yesterday
eating Apple Hill Farms eggs,
sunny-side up,
Aunt Jemima's waffles with Blue Bonnet
Margarine and Mom's
homemade raspberry jelly,
Quaker Oats and cream
with Nestle's hot chocolate
when Rob choked
on a marshmallow.
Dad just scooped him out of his highchair
and turned him upside down.
Rob was all
red and white and
tears slipped off his cheeks
like little spoons.

Trek

Winter nights, nine,
I helped my blind father
lock up our store—the right

click in the door
by twin gas pumps
(their white-red globes—"Kendall")—

angle around cars in our icy
parking lot, then walk
to our house on the path

shoveled through high drifts,
caramel-colored money bag
hung from his wrist,

moonlight on an endless stretch of snow
and the white, crossed
beams of our clothes pole.

Property

Our back porch, I discover from the yard,
is caving in;
eaves troughs rust in the grass.
What defines the limits of this house?
Spirea takes over the living room;
rain attacking the neighbor's tin roof
advances this way.

I stand on the back steps,
smell the rain, and through her screen,
the match Mother lights
to cook supper.

She comes to the door,
and we talk about
Bradley's acres of dark winter wheat, growing
farther from us
across the newly widened road.

We used to own the place next door—
my father's, his father's grocery,
my sister's and brother's early apartments;
I've never given it up.
An old Pepsi Cola sign
shines from the upstairs window in the barn.
We claim the heavy
peonies nodding across the line,
elegant iris we planted
rise in their yard.

Stories from the Southern Tier

1

When the Genesee was rising
back in June
people touring Letchworth Park
stopping to dine at the Glen Iris Inn
saw cows churning over
the Middle Falls.

2

River banks collapsed near Fillmore
though one bridge, like a monument to the road,
stood in the sediment's swirl
on its strong pillars.

3

A barn, its foundation undermined,
floated down the rage
and landed square on the bridge.
And inside the barn
after the flood,
somebody found a calf
chewing in its stall,
still surrounded by hay.

Miss Weld

"Emma S. Weld," you always signed your name
in books you loaned,
on jar labels of peaches
for deliverance after Sunday School.
Your voice shook in a violent alto
above the bright blue hymnal;
your prayers, too long, took us all in.

Lunch at your house
was a special occasion;
a former home economics teacher,
you didn't invite just anyone.
We ate by the pot-bellied stove in the dining room,
but later you opened the parlor doors
and showed me the stained glass window
bright purple and red over the stairs.
Then, ice cream in cut glass bowls.
Dust in every cut outlined the rim too perfectly.

Tonight, clumps of dirt
settle around your coffin
like small bunches of grapes,
alveoli.

The Sunday School collected
over thirty dollars in your memory:
we'll purchase our first Communion set,
the silver tray, the little glasses.
Come to the first service.

Tonight, with a newer friend,
ate orange rice casserole,
cider and red tea
before we went to church.

At the service, each one sang God's praise
a separate song, a separate key,
the Bread,
moist between my teeth
and clear,
the Wine
spreading in my lungs, Miss Weld
like lavender.

Spaulding's

A good long time
since Joyce Spaulding has been gone,
but let me walk into Newberry's in Batavia,
or grade an essay comparing Macy's with K-Mart,
and she appears in the aisle,
halted in the middle of her ambling gait,
some piece of merchandise slung over her arm,
saying, *Gawd, you again?*

And how are Dawn, Michelle, and Deborah, I launch,
her daughters, my childhood cronies,
raised on books and Pepsi;
how are Faye, Wanda, Gene, Ben, Kenneth,
and how are
you, beyond all your suffering?

Her house, always under construction,
needed a bedroom downstairs,
a warmer bathroom—
and I remember us girls at breakfasts—
Hershey's swirling like pinwheels
through large
glasses of
her dad's fresh cow's milk—
and one supper table,
my standing up to reach something
while she sat there, asking,
"Do you stand that way at your house?"

Finally she sewed me a dress,
organdy, chartreuse,
with a sash, and high
ruffles around the arm openings,
for Children's Day—same pattern as her girls'.

In the living room, her daughters shouted
when I spent the night,
"Down in front!"
or, "You're a better door than a window!"
so they could watch *The Millionaire.*

And on that T.V. sat a growling
panther, flanks
silvery in the lamp's reflection,
while from tiny chains,
like four-square
slats of Venetian blind,
dropped down, as if suspended,
its green shade—bright, extensive.

The Discovery

"Sometimes," Mother told me
"birds fall down our old chimney,
you can hear them fluttering in the pipe;
then I open the lid of the old wood stove
on the side of the range, and they fly up;
they go for light,
first to the window—
I push them along the wall with a broom,
they find the door, and out.
Sometimes they don't fly up, though;
I don't know where they go."

Cleaning deep inside her oven,
lifting a kind of trap door
my sick mother didn't know was there,
I found four dead birds
black and stiff
their small white bones charred.

I labored to clean them out,
and wondered what law their lives fulfilled—
flying for warmth, or just flying;
their days seemed unkindly measured,
and I placed them in a paper bag
under a tree behind our old chicken coop
like a broken treasure.

Summons

Early June and heavy syringa
seeps through the screen
into Mother's living room;
the porch steps, soft, splintered,
are more decayed than ever;
under the roof
two swallows debate
rights to an old nest;
and calling me away,
in the far, front corner,
the wild red rose again.

Bookcase

1

With pressure and
strong soap,
the dark stain, residue of smoke,
of fire that almost
claimed Mother's house,
washes off
this bookcase my father built.

2

It had stood next to the china cupboard
in the dining room,
four shelves stacked with
my parents' hardbacks,
old texts from several children's
college days, books for girls:
Long's English Literature,
The Good Earth, East of Eden,
The Sermons of Peter Marshall,
The Greek Way to Western Civilization,
Man and His Symbols,
Anne of Green Gables,
Heidi.

3

In a few more minutes,
the firemen told us,
the fire would have hit
"the cross-over point,"
the whole place exploding in flame—
Dad had died years before,
Mother was escorted out quickly—

but they controlled it,
climbing in upstairs windows,
breaking down the bannister,
flooding the rooms with water.

4
On its top three doilies used to display
decorations Mother never changed:
a Dutch boy planter; a green, oblong vase,
a copper, toy lantern;
over it hung
a mirror, outlined
with white flowers
my sisters faced nightly
setting their hair in pin curls.

5
As I scrub,
the hard wood asserts
its wavy grain,
and crossing it,
curves of bobby pins,
their pyramidal lines preserved here,
burned into the wood
like hieroglyphs.

Stuck paper peels off
one of the lower shelves,
but not all of the print
of ads, from flyleaves
in the backs of unbound books;
I can read some of the fragments,
backwards.

6

Then, months after the fire,
in the bitter winter
season, following Mother's death,
five adult children entered
the house,
cold ashes everywhere,
and dealt with the black
furniture and objects.

7

And I think of Dad measuring these boards
for that particular space,
inserting them in their cut out
grooves, nailing
the bookcase together;
and of Mother loading it up, arranging
books on its shelves for years,
whatever they had gathered from the world
to help them set
a house in order.

May Third

Oh, wild lilac,
you toss up a beautiful
purple to strong wind
on this cool spring evening
the sadness of which
one can scarcely capture.

Tapestry

The unicorn who
is spotted, whose
horn absorbs poison
from the fountain of life, who
is cruelly surrounded
by hunters and dogs
and cannot escape though he
wounds a hound;
the unicorn who
captured is coaxed
to the marriage feast, who
is bound to a pomegranate
in a small space, how
when he rears
though tied to that tree
does he rejoice!

II

The Giraffe

head nubs like
the horned owl's,
ambiguous llama face
and always chewing

ears pointed
yet delicately cupped
as light shells
singing on the coast

her long neck
steady
acquiescent yes,
her walk on slender limbs
easy as the swan's gliding when she
moves so slightly the light
foot to turn around

back home in the plains
the thornbush
country of Kenya, Ethiopia
hunting leaves and just ripe
twigs of acacia trees

then can kick
use the neck, club, no
race across the ground,
gain speed

now licks
the steel rail's post
scratches her length
on spring's bare maple

long thought never
to utter a
sound but does

A Guide Leads a Tour of the Plantation House in Barbados, Built in 1650

Correct, it's the oldest house on the island,
once a master's,
most—you'll understand I say, thankfully—
of the original structure is gone:
the cast iron kitchen, the back laundry room;
those white beams above us, their fussy molding,
never my taste—remains;
three-foot walls still make good insulation.

Wine cooler, sideboard
in the dining room to your left—
yes, the seventeenth-century pieces
you find interesting;
the china setting is later,
the table's our native mahogany, Barbadian.
That's one of three fireplaces the English laid
before they realized we didn't need them.

Striking? The bold bouquets—
orange, mauve, pink hibiscus from our gardens—
I make them every day;
hibiscus last just that long—outside, in;
no beauty's lost in picking them.

And here in this room, our shop,
this inventory behind glass lists slaves;
all had to be accounted for—
children, the disabled,
those too old to work—
see, Lucy's listed worth $20,
and these, as $0.

See those articles there on the mannequin—
the bracelet, gray dress, and large-pocketed apron
worn by a slave?
I came to work early one day last week
and tried them on;
no, of course, I'm not allowed—
I can't tell you the weakness I felt,
then rage. I felt like a vapor.
Can you imagine endless days here
when this breeze wouldn't cool,
God's sun not shine for your pleasure?
Right, it's difficult.

Let's move along . . .
in this next room, the large den,
rests "a gentleman's chair," last century;
you can see how a man could sidle in here,
put up his feet, sit
read his morning paper,
and later prop his book on this rack,
and to stack his tray, order lunch or tea—
and anything else he wanted
from the women servants—
my great grandmother passed down stories
I begin to understand now.

Here's a picture of the present owner,
plus six generations before him;
we used to show his rooms upstairs,
but tourists lifted an ivory comb, sterling pieces.
Yes, a working plantation—
slaves were freed in 1834, gradually—
indentured, underpaid.

When you go out back—careful,
down these high, ancient steps—don't lean on or touch
that spiny tree, same age as the house;
barbs you can't see 'til they stab you
shadow its bark.

Walk through those gates to the barn—
the history of machinery used for sugaring;
no, no tips for me on my last day—
and here's a device, cut in this stone wall,
original with the house, yet still, amazingly,
as though anything here could be, useful;
see those hollows in the stone?
the curved shapes inside like urns?
rain would seep
through successive
limestone containers,
until the planters collected
in this lowest one,
water,
—Here, sample some—
relieved of its debris, pure
as any of us might desire.

The Pledge

Alain dreams down occasionally
into the oilcloth and mahogany kitchen
where Papa has sprinkled rum
on biscuits and flan,
and offers it to guests,
where his mother smiles her approval
and talks on.

He knows the plan of this house he wants
to keep, to pass on,
how the screened porch encloses its north side
where Flica, the ancient Pekingese, rests,
how the rooms flow into each other,
and the outside, vine-covered stairs lead down
into his boyhood room
where his covenant with God is engraved
in the stone wall:
outside his wrought iron door,
the path where the dogs keep watch
leads to the yard where last spring,
just one year after his mother died,
he cut back the over-hanging bamboo branches;
higher up, as though from the mountains in Boutellier,
he can see how the front steps
lead, eventually, into the harbor on the west,
while the east side fronts
a less accessible side of the island.
Though the government decrees
the land shall return to its countrymen
and none of this will be his,
he leaves his children,
the side of his sleeping wife with child
to dream down to something a man can still own:
the well-marked place
in the foundation of the house
one takes from and may return.

Where We Lived

It was dark
It was bleak
It was bad news
even in Spring Lake
during The War

My brother aboard a fleet
minesweeper in the South Pacific—
Black men given all the worst jobs
in all the worst places—
like poor Whites from the South,
"the expendable"

Our yards were decked—
blue star, a man in the Service,
gold star, a man killed. Young,
my emotions like bullets, I'd cry
or race across the street to escape
a flowered wreath on a door

Even his coming home on furlough
saddened us:
silent, he would have to return
to where, he exploded thirty years later
at a family picnic, he was alien
from himself

Once, on leave, he created
a fishpond back of our house—
lined it with red cement,
filled it with stripes
of goldfish forever darting.

Musings from the Road; Looking Across a Spring Hillside

For Ruth and Sean, severely wounded in Iraq

*. . . and they shall beat their swords into plowshares,
and their spears into pruning hooks; nation shall not lift
up sword against nation, neither shall they learn war
anymore; but they shall sit every man under his vine
and under his fig tree . . .*

Micah 4:3b–4a

The brown field is a shawl
across a woman's shoulders,
this sunset, even light
keens from the curve of the horizon:

No call for an enemy
bullet through her son's
neck and back—
seedlings grip long furrows,
like dark stitches, his body.

New grain roots,
like the cauterized
artery re-rooted
his heart in that rich texture;
his ripped muscle slowly
relearns "trapezius," original
lay of the land—

In sowing and reaping,
not in brandishing destruction, what
new fruit, what new thread, what promise.

Road to Emmaus

There have been crucifixions, too,
in our town—innocents
gunned down in their doorways
or in school halls; or radiation's
black outlines, three crosses
marked a sister's chest: no wonder
we walk in quiet rage, musing.

And who, on this road, will join us,
seeming unaware
of the worst news in the neighborhood,
but spelling out the history of the prophets
and a future:
    Ought not Christ to have suffered these things
    and to enter into his glory?
Could our hearts still burn within us?

Will we ask the stranger to stay?
Break bread? And how
will our well-hammered and nailed
kitchens and bedrooms appear to us
when we understand who he is
just as he steals away?

III

Arrival

Children forsake their favorite fruit,
The teakettle sings the rooster mute:
So runs the pleasing disarray
Of no quite ordinary Day.
Such Honor has informed the barn
As turns the whole world upside down;
Joseph strides to swift from shy. Olives
Bend to hear Christ's lullaby.

At Christ's Birth

a small bird
bore up rafters
on its wings

a weanling calf
settled in the straw

there was a sound
almost impossible
as fontanel
parting crystal

The Forerunner

Like the son
of struck dumb
Zacharias
our best words
cry in the wilderness

And come unseemly dressed
confusedly subject
to metaphor

John
of the camel's hair and leather
was not
that Lamb
that Light
that Word

So, for his preambling
paradox did:
after me
a follower
comes before

And cosmic irony:
Jordan man
revealing
the sponsor of the Holy Ghost
and fire

Allegorization:
the groomsman joys
to hear the bridegroom's voice

Oh, symbol-form grow great
oh, symbol
less

'Til lovely
(as in pauses)

The Word
makes flesh
transcend itself

And John
his dearest speaker knows
what death it is to call
for priests and kings

So execution strikes—

But benediction
He comes
a blaze on water
Breath on wings

Memorials

Yes, I indulged the moment:
setting my white heirloom box
next to his plate
at Simon's dull table;
placing my hand on his hair
to anoint his head with ointment—
the room awoke, wavered
in perfume.

His friends complained:
Extravagance.
But how could I have spread thin
what ounce of wealth I owned?
I had watched this man
heal the blind and maimed,
heard him speak—
I was making amends for my doom.

And for his, he said,
though I wasn't foreseeing a burial—
I've yet to understand;
we all die, I mean—eventually,
collapse,
we towers
of bone.

To Chirst's Colt

Was there some ivory in your bone,
Or did your golden limbs cast such a hue
That He transformed you to His glistening throne?
Or was it that His Grace had saddled you?

Good Friday Night, Covering the Pansies

The gardener warned, "Too soon to put them in."
Desiring them, I'll need to keep close track
Of cold; each face, like His, will fold like sin
On trial, as on a wooden rack
Outside a market—merchants don't care if some
Are lost. I'll find a covering fine as gauze,
Make sure to cover every vulnerable one—
Nature shows little mercy in its laws.

That night, we left the church in silence, dark,
The moon round as a wafer or a tarnished dime;
The Isaiah candle by the pulpit kept one spark.
Home—the chill reminded me of time
To check the claim of frost, ashes, dirt. Light bands
Of cloth we laid redressed the garden like a shirt.

Angelus

Oh, Bell that rings the Angelus,
You are the Angelus;
The call to Prayer, a Prayer,
The Ringer of the Bell, a Capital
Who, What, Where.

Since God was born one morning,
The Best of When and Why,
Even Sparrows gain a Tower's Height
At noontime,
Soaring by.

Smithy, Smith, and Ground will Flower
Resurrection Strong. God's Statement, Bold
And Blatant, shapes the Mute
And Mumbling into Song.

Lord, Let Light

glance from every washed
plate, from green drainer or white
stove, let light
shine out at odd
angles, from each clattering
risk I take even
from this small
here, open
windows, let the sun
spark fire near
or far, when I won't
throw open my door
let my elbows un-
hinge, poorest visitors, your visitants
in, let dead center
(like yours) be glory, oh world's
weeping wall.

A Bee

A bee,
Interestingly,

Is a membrane
Nerved with stuff
That lifts a tiger body
A golden cuff
A head with onyx eyes

And carries him
To where a whisker limb
Pulls a field
Of clover
Down.

A cell
May create a Canaan in its swell.

Trying to Help the Feisty Young Music Teacher Vest Junior Choir, Palm Sunday

"You're labeling the children's hangers wrong—
Those little scraps of paper—on the floor . . ."
    "Names/numbers on the rack, as all along . . ."
"Your robing's chaos." *"Well, this job's a bore."*

God told two unnamed men, "Go, loose a colt."
Mundane. The need: simply to toe the line.
"What's going on?" They answered with God's quote.
Just so—the Kingdom comes. Grapes yield their wine.

"This robe's not mine—too tight!" "Over there's #10."
*(Some word, this quick rehearsal could be lost.
But I'll be damned if I'll do this again.)*

New tape. The names cleaned up. What cost?
This teacher's qualified, creative, strong—
And some child here may clothe a self with song.

This Christmas

we must know Him differently—
as though a bell rose
from the baby's face.

The tale of miracle is not enough,
nor are softly countenanced figurines
bedded down in imported straw
by fountain centers of outlying malls.

It must be written anew;
we must see all our ingenuities of metal
rising composite from flesh
as though our weapons have been redeemed.

We must hear in sirens
fallen petals.
Think, there are other ways it could mean.

IV

Conundrum

This winter night's cornering wind,
like a rising dough no one's kneading,
is getting away
with
itself.

Dream

In my dream
I visited you,
late afternoon,
and you weren't dressed;
you were cooking a second lunch
because at noon you'd eaten
a family of chocolate bars in desperation.
Why didn't you call? I asked.
You said you couldn't have borne
not finding me home.

Early morning,
and my head's heavy as a drunk's
with the frailty of human consciousness.
I'm stupidly sorry for all my harsh words;
no snubbing seems pert or smart.
If I could catch
the train tressling by outside,
I'd knock on your back door
like a hobo.

Role of Nonsense

Remember Poor Tom,
frog, toad,
tadpole eater
that in the fury of his heart
when the foul fiend rages
eats cow dung for salads,
drinks slime,
and is whipped from post to post;
it's just plain sad,
and my only friend peeked
out from behind a pillar,
playing an original game
in the afternoon,
and I couldn't talk to him—
I was busy, wasn't I?
and didn't have time.
Even my shyest student,
Don't you know
that you
who always refuse
to look me in the eye
could be comfort to me now,
traipsing across the school ground
with your camera,
not even saying hello,
out taking pictures, I guess
of the autumn leaves?
Oh, everything's crest-
fallen, and at the turn of a thought
one could be ill or well;
nobody answers the ad in the newspaper,
so Bob, I just want to know
can you help me sell
these green walnuts
I once had time
to gather by the pail?

Leaving Work, I Spot a Deer Crossing Dominican Drive

I slow up,
recall my unsettled mind,
in the middle of the driving, Stop:

Note the doe's flowing coat, the angling
face forms, the familiar tail, hung
in its own perfect frame;
when she halts, so briefly
at the fence guarding the woods,
take in the easy
energy she musters
to lift both front hooves over
the fence, then
the back ones—and see how a valley
has been slowly hollowed out
through the impassable mountains.

In Sydney Mount's Painting, Named *The Painter's Triumph*

an artist's hair flies
from his face;
swinging his palette and brush out
behind him, he keeps his eyes glued
to his just-finished painting—

beside him, a farmer, slightly
bent, hands on overalled knees,
leans joyfully into that work
where he sees, for himself,
light breaking!

in a small
oval portrait behind the farmer,
Apollo, green-garlanded, turns his aquiline
nose away in disgust
at this sun-flooded moment before him.

Reading a Student's Paper

Marion, on her ladder,
pasting flowers—
I'm trying to read just
that carefully—
my scribble on the page
accurate, suggestions—
to improve a house, its walls—
the paper, tight against
the ceiling, a brush over
the vines, the matching,
catching
a curve off the line
of thought, plurals,
possessives, whose
entitlement is this?
All of us
glad, especially Mother,
a job done,
walls, tended—a new place to be,
to walk through—to
the columns supporting
the front porch—Marion later
spread the story, how she knew—
from down the road—
sparrows singing extra clearly
and loudly in our bushes
the morning
my brother
was born.

Redeemed Afternoon

For my sister Carol

After boredom, after quarrels,
listing the extent
you're taking care of yourself, or not,
after heels dug in
like the only existing
part of our body,

An actual walk together
through your own acres of woods out back,
far as we can go
along the stony ridges,
you, with your walking stick
in this terrain I'd forgotten,
its deep, stream-worn ravines,
these lookout heights,
slim trees, and exposed, white roots—

You wished you could record
my lying prone on the damp ground
photographing here Spring's barely
noticeable spot of color:
a pair
of dog-toothed yellow violets.

Visiting My Elder Sister, Carol
Western New York, Rhubarb Time

It's rare this season—no rain;
your local nursery, closed.
Jersey farm stands had received no deliveries—
Today, you're the third who's asked.

Yet these pale and pink-veined
stalks we found together,
tossing their mad, green fronds

against the relic of a rusted pump
at your field's edge—
and which, you said, sampling,
tasted *dead dry*—

sliced in little crescents,
are soaking up water and sweetener
in this simmering pan, and dissolving

like knobby knuckles into fresh, red sinews
pouring out their nurture
from that parched, abandoned plot
we plucked them from.

Energy Flow

Out the window, against the overcast
landscape of western New York,
several lines of poles with insulators rise
from a high-functioning energy transmitting station.

In here, the doctor deftly
inserts acupuncture needles,
little slips of silver
coated with sky-blue, plastic tips,
into your hands, feet, knee, hip,
and finally along the longitude
of your painful back.
How do I look? You ask me.
Like a picture of glinting masts
lost in a strange sea, I don't tell you.

Soon, you can sleep,
the doctor compassing his stated goals:
rebalancing chi, removing
its obstructions—whatever blocked it.
Awake, you report, in time, as he instructed,
a small quake in your subcutaneous tissue,
energy's smooth flow returning.

On a barn roof nearby
partly stripped of its shingles,
a map of my world emerges: wide oceans
and continents' coastlines, their recognizable edges.

Captain's Chair

A cupcake rises
out of the kitchen table:
dark mound and white squiggle,
a daily treat from my father's store;
I sit in his captain's chair
spilling over to Mother
about my day at school.

This is the chair
that's on the road today
coming home to me
from a town on Lake Michigan;
a black scar's hollowed into it,
base of the second spindle,
where, after stoking the wood fire
in the side of our kitchen stove
yet another cold morning,
my father placed his burning glove.

He called us to come quickly
from our beds;
blind, he couldn't know
where the whorls of smoke
were coming from—
and Mother told him
he could not tend that fire anymore.

I can see my brother
bearing that oak chair across his yard,
loading it deep into the dark trailer,
securing the cords to hold it
tight as possible.

This Is the Picture of Mother on the Path
Between Our House and Store

The store's as stark
as a Shaker meeting house,
shades in its back room windows,
half drawn;
beyond it, across the road,
snow defines the roof
of Metzler's barn and shed;
beside it, a '57 Dodge
divides our shoveled lot,
a path curves through the huge drift
between our store and house,
and Mother in the foreground, on the path,
no boots pulled on,
just shoes in the tracked slush,
hands in her pocket, draws her coat
around her in the wind.
Her hair around her kerchief blows back;
her eyes, behind gold-rimmed glasses,
half close.

Pulling crosswise at the picture
is such a smile shaping her face
that a son must be
on leave from the Armed Forces,
or grandchildren at play in snow,
or she walks to the store to add
something to dinner,
and someone has asked her to
turn in the middle of the errand—*Hey,
Ma*—and discovered her at home
with thoughts in her mind
or pleasures
as ray out
from her own time, her place.

End of a Job

I feel like one,
who admiring her face
in a mirror,
had hoped to find
in her bright room,
a mirror, too,
behind:
depth, no end
those familiar mirrors
reflecting her
over and
over again—
like one, who
appearing whole there once,
then, in outline,
fears that now (through some fault
in quicksilver
or trick of the eye) she's become invisible

gone

This uprootedness
makes me
grope beyond the water's
mirror surface—
more than a sapling,
I stretch through my native
underground
to find once more
where,
and how deep
the
pools
are.

V

Nineteenth-Century Dream

You woke me so gently
with your kisses and caress,
I remembered
(or thought I did)
the meadow in bloom
beside the train and rail;
Queen Anne's lace
beside a burning coal.

Sampler

Gentle,
the Amish
girls born
into black bonnets and tunics,
into white aprons;
they learn sewing
at closed windows,
eyes below white muslin
reflecting on light—
how clear the Creation;
learn riding early
in open buggies
eyes below white muslin
learning the roads—
the fields are not black,
the soil, brown, loosening
returns the dark gaze.
They marry in gray
and please young husbands
taking in the dark eyes,
then honeymoon round
for neighborhood gifts
until home, they are home
proud in black aprons
proud to be making patterns,
making banquets:
the raising of barns,
the tying of quilts,
pails scrubbed silver,
bread rising daily.

Above the kitchen stove,
their bedroom faces
the full barn, so evening fires
may be spotted,
and here, afternoons, they sing
to the bloomed cherry grain of cradles.
Their sons are taken by fathers and land,
their daughters by households.
Home is Sunday's meeting place:
a cloth
a hymn
a communion,
until, second brides,
they bear
white aprons to the grave,
smoothed with hands
made as of ribs,
and wait for the wand of God.

Here, in Hinckley, Ohio

Capistrano's not the only place
to make the news,
with their swallows,
small, delicate birds:
we celebrate here, in Hinckley, too—
and Welcome.
Why commemorate the buzzards' return?
And why not?
Shiny as onyx, sleek—sure
they eat carrion, but tell me—
who, in some form or other, doesn't?
And, given the chance,
they'll walk right into our picnic
pluck choice cake
from our white linen tables
and the very best macaroons;
they're not fussy.

But that's not all
we're celebrating here today.
Wait 'til you see my daughter—
"an unclaimed blessing" neighbors called her,
meaning "left-over." Who noticed
her shy beauty? Able, though, like these first
spring flowers.
And the groom—a fine man
who's made the rounds for years—
won't he be struttin' at the reception
in his black coat and tails!

Inland, Lancaster County

This morning in Mt. Joy
roosters crisply crow,
doves define soft songs,
but I lie limp
as the cloth
that Esther,
downstairs,
clothed in her prayer cap,
draws across the counter
where she cracks
eggs, slices spuds
for us, her overnight guests.

I hurt you,
let the sun go down
on our distress:
all flesh,
my back is slung
like a remnant braided
in bad times
for the dreariest rug.

Back home, I think, in Manhattan,
traffic, synchronized by lights,
moves peaceably
on its grid of streets;
I could weave to the East River,
wrap my hands around a rail,
gaze out at barges,
large, dark, nebulous
in mist—unkindness casts haze like this—
but guided by a red, headstrong
tug—*Christ, pull my sin*
and our sadness to sea,
dawn's ocean of mercy,
Atlantic.

Hat

Your hand on my forehead is a cloche,
high fashion; or tipped to one side,
a jaunty beret;
on my face, your hand, like a veil,
moves with slight changes in the weather;
your hand on my skull
is a prayer cap.

First Cousins

When Jerome leapt
out of his car
(first visit to our new house)
we ran to greet him—
and pennies
kept dropping
out of his pockets
onto the driveway,
and we got to laughing
because we'd pick them up,
fingers clamping them,
and reinsert them,
hoping for better luck—
that the holes
in some pockets, at least,
might be missed,
or not
there—
but no,
they'd stream down again,
fierce pennies
gleaming on the pavement.
And you have to know Jerome,
tall, sophisticated, an artist,
how he's laughing uncontrollably,
leaning over the hood
of his jalopy, embarrassed.

Then, for a gift,
he pulls out this bag
of peaches—
and they're bleeding through,
wet, coppery,
and he tells how he
picked them last night
so they'd be ready,
and they're ripe all right in August,
ripening more, maybe
in the steaming car.

And we're in the kitchen by now,
Jerome urging us to
please taste the peaches,
they're delicious,
from trees he planted himself,
from pits—
and he says,
thumbs hooked in his pockets,
gazing out the back window,
"Perhaps one could do worse,"
so I'm cutting off
the bruised parts
and we're all lighting
into gold, gouged
spheres, our chins
dripping, best
fruit we ever tasted.

The Occurrence (Almost)

Received in a letter from Maria, bored in the country

Yesterday, in the village of Warsaw, New York,
slipping down East Hill lickety-split
a banana truck tipped over.

(Same hill where the watermelon truck,
a few months ago when I wasn't here,
slipped a gear, tipped over,
spilling watermelons down into town;
they tumbled through traffic lights—red or green
and finally crashed into a house
filling its cellar
with a foot and a half of watermelon juice.)

Anyhow, this bananas truck driver
was only fined $100.00:
$50 for crossing the yellow line,
$50 for carrying too much weight.

He was carrying 18 T of bananas;
but not one of them
fell off of the truck.

The Usual

Those who have not experienced the glow engendered
on one's entering the coffee shop, and having the server inquire,
"the Usual?" are poor indeed.

For who wants to stay home? The comfort of
domesticity may be great, indeed, but it is not convivial.

No, the Idle Hour, Coffee Corner, Coffee Cup,
where even the stranger may still find himself addressed
as "Hon"—that is the place for me.

David Mamet

One always knows what to expect
in a diner—with a name like Fireside,
The Rainbow, or Chester—
broad muffins shining in clear wrap
by the counter juke box
checked with all the letters
of the alphabet and numbers—1–0;
ketchup; a sugar dispenser—
silver, its top flap;
a black cubed,
open-mouthed
napkin holder.

The decor will never
betray you—
look for a fake
brick wall; coach lamps
outside restrooms,
out-of-scale chandeliers,
spider plants,
a mighty-shouldered beverage dispenser,

half cantaloupes
peaked,
look for the orbiting cakes.

Always, at the salad bar
flaking chunks
of feta cheese,
and something—like tapioca—
wrapped in leaves;
a swirl of orange
curls in the neighboring dressing;
lettuce, tomatoes, onions shine
colorful as Christmas.

On your placemat, fantasies—
for Custom T-Shirt Printing,
Prestige Volvo,
affordable
auto insurance for Jersey drivers,
silk screening at The Harbor,
Singing Strings School in Livingston—
the Suzuki approach to violin, viola, violin-cello.

Not that rumors of life gone wrong
don't leak in—
newspapers at the door
rack up local and foreign murders;
a diagram on the wall
instructs us, step by step
in the Heimlich.

Nonetheless, one sometimes wishes
for all the Bible's
splendid descriptions,
for all the Saints' visions,
paradise could be like this—
something instantly recognizable
by eye or hand—
graspable
as a caramel or brown
coffee decanter,
or a silver-mounded salt
or pepper shaker
at a booth
or a full, round table,
where, when you walk in
through Windexed glass doors,
and are seated,
hungry, expectant,
the waitress, alert,
note pad ready,
pencil carried
at some familiar angle
extending through space and time
sings out
in four clear tones,
"What can I get you, Hon?"

One Early Morning Commuter Bus Ride
I'm Unable to Find a Desired Seat, Alone

Someone
must love
this dull stranger beside me,
flesh slouched
forward on his face,
chin resting on the nub
of a tie,
white hair pushed back—
the wearing of ring,
a watch,
a thin blue stripe in his suit—
and red—
Threadings to match
many shirts, the salesman must have said.
Then, I'll go with this.
The *Star Ledger* molds to his lap.

Out the
generous window
lofty
plate-like clouds,
uniform row descending
upon row,
taper to
a point
at the horizon—
one silver line streams out of La Guardia—
the veiled
sun is a heart,
and on Route 3
we're swimming together toward the Tunnel
under the lustrous belly
of a vast, scaled fish.

Poetic Justice/Strip Mall

"Did you hit my car?" The woman
had appeared between her glossy
yellow Nissan tank
and my 4-cylinder, old, tan
Camry. From the sidewalk
in front of the ice cream parlor
I thought hard.
"I felt a jolt," she added. "You mean,"
I mustered, "with my door?"
She was examining
the bright side of the universe
for a slit.
Her eyes were wide. From the sidewalk's
safety, "I try to be careful," I said.

Inside, I ordered
my usual—a medium lemon
chiffon yogurt cone.
"Is this too big? Do you need
a cup before it topples?
I must be the world's most neurotic
store owner. I always worry—
this stuff's to eat, not for people's
coats. The kids
that work for me, they
couldn't care less—if it lands
on the floor, people's fingers . . .
wherever—can I help you
with that purse zipper?
Here's a stack of napkins—got them?
and a serving spoon,
when that sucker starts to roll, just
give it a good whack."

Dishes in the Sink

Dishes in the sink cannot
be transformed by any act
of imagination:
they are not a still life,
abstract design,
nor a playful Klee;
not part of the grand
scheme of things, beginning
with the great platter of sky
flecked with sweet crumbs of cloud.

Even rinsed and ready
for the immaculate
gullet of the dishwasher
only an inch away,
they are growing
what only scientists
and the well-read can name.
God declaring them good
will not cut it.

No, dirty dishes will always be
a sign of shame—
of work that must be done,
of the lazy man who's misplaced
his priorities as often as his glasses,
of the woman, rushing
herself or her children
to a giant, greasy butter dish of a bus—
something ranked right up there
with piles of clothes left covering the floor
and the sparkling morning's
unmade bed.

Sale: Mattress and Box Springs

Our new, high bed has thrown
everything off; one-third
the way to the ceiling,
it looms.

My husband, The Emperor,
peruses *The Times*
perched far above
our burnished, now
buried, maple headboard.

I'm an entrenched Princess.
The height of "standard" grew
when, for decades, we were napping.
More is less.

We've lost that
"Colonial" feeling—though we propped
up the rest of the bedroom set on bricks,
and raised all the portraits.

We share the ceiling—
without a skylight—
and our "raised Cape" now drapes,
like a Mogul's bathrobe-for-two, around us.

The bill reads, *Not exchangeable.*
Elegance isn't all it's cracked up to be.
We're sleeping unevenly, the odds
stacked against ourselves.

Stage of Life

I hear silence—and I think she . . .
                   (Why is he)
                          must be giving up
     (running so fast up the)
                    because she had been so tired, and
    (stairs—he planned to)
                        wanted to go upstairs
    (draw in the)
                            too early—
  (basement—or are we)
                              Are you
(simply being robbed?) Are you o.k.?   o.k.?

Lovliest of Cacti, the Ocotillo Now

Loveliest of cacti, the ocotillo now
Extends slim lines, as does my brow,
And stands inside the cycle track
Its red flowers clear as bric-a-brac.

Now, of my threescore years and ten,
"*New forty*" will not come again,
And take from seventy springs threescore,
It only leaves me (gulp!) ten more.

And since to squint at things in bloom
Was futile from inside my room,
Around the ocotillo I have spun
To feel the desert drenched with sun.

Just to See Alice

Just to see Alice, 85,
disembark from her neighbor's car
in her pink and blue dress, bright
against leaves—russet, brown,
just to see her newly curled hair,
just to see her, carpet bag-like
purse in hand, achieve
the black-topped driveway's
20-degree incline
through her and Grant's leaf-free
fertilized lawn,
just to see her
turn the corner, make the
wooden steps
to the small deck, square,
just to see her insert
the key in the latch
and push open
her own kitchen door.

Be

a body in space, dimensional
like the flowering
pear that sets to right
suburbs in spring

Trunks focus, sun
spills; be
light in wide diffusion
against those slats of cloud

What shapes nothing
takes
among the white
blossoms! Breathe, recede—see now
what wind begins to blow

Phone Connection

For my dear friend Sandi

You are backing away, you tell me
from your picture window, to capture—
discovering your feeder—sudden
cardinals against fresh snow

Here, broad-winged buds of red amaryllis
perched before white lace curtains
absorb far-flung
scatterings of light

Why Forrest K. Moses Didn't Enjoy Painting on Pottery, Though He Did It for Family and Friends

When you paint on a vessel
such as a jug,
you have to employ foresight
and trust luck
to join the scene's ends:
sledders may not run
into your beginning line;
a woman must be waving, not out
at the pot's owner,
but at native folk, leaving;
mountains, clouds, ground,
as theology links here
with there, have to join.
Don't start under the spout,
a likely spot;
rather, between the spout
(an imaginary line)
and the wire handle's clay holder
is fine;
warm up easy with white, a pine—
the broadside's dangerous for beginners:
picture that as a single scene.
Then,
yellow cornstalks X-ing the snow
should sweep, move—
never lose a wide space to nothing but snow;
don't crowd
barns, groceries; blue, red.
Coming round
sighting your original evergreen,
retire somewhere shy
of the three sledders
in primary caps, bright sweaters,
coasting the grade
in front of the mustard house
and the woman waving
good-bye.

About the Author

Sandra R. Duguid was born and raised in rural western New York, outside Batavia, and some of her poems derive from that rural setting. She received a B.A. from Houghton College. She has an M.A. in Creative Writing from Johns Hopkins University and a Ph.D. in English from the University of Buffalo, where she wrote her dissertation on the fiction of Harriet Beecher Stowe.

She has taught literature, composition, and creative writing at colleges in the New York/New Jersey metropolitan area and at East Stroudsburg University in Pennsylvania. She was Assistant Director of the Academic Support Center at Caldwell College in Caldwell, New Jersey, managing the Writing Center for seven years. She retired in summer, 2010, to devote more time to writing.

She was awarded a Fellowship in Poetry from the New Jersey State Council on the Arts and was invited to read her poetry in a Geraldine R. Dodge Poetry Festival. She has also read her poems in colleges, several reading series in New Jersey, and in bookstores. One of her poems received honorable mention in the Allen Ginsberg Poetry Contest, sponsored by Passaic County Community College, and her poem "Road to Emmaus" received a prize in a contest sponsored by Calvin College. She lives in New Jersey with her husband, Henry Gerstman.